THE MYSTERIES OF LIGHT

The Bible and the New Luminous Mysteries

Roland J. Faley

Paulist Press
New York/Mahwah, N.J.

Cover design by Cynthia Dunne
Book design by Lynn Else

Library of Congress Cataloging-in-Publication Data

Faley, Roland J. (Roland James), 1930–
    The mysteries of light : the Bible and the new luminous mysteries / Roland J. Faley.
        p. cm.
    Includes bibliographical references.
    ISBN 0-8091-4293-7 (alk. paper)
    1. Mysteries of the Rosary. 2. Bible. N.T. Gospels—Criticism, interpretation, etc. I. Title.

    BT303 .F15 2005
    242'.74—dc22

                                                                2004013310

Published by Paulist Press
997 Macarthur Boulevard
Mahwah, New Jersey 07430

www.paulistpress.com

Printed and bound in the
United States of America

Contents

Preface

*I*n October 2002, Pope John Paul II added five additional mysteries to the Rosary, complementing the fifteen which have been in possession for centuries. This book is an attempt to look at each of these mysteries in the light of contemporary biblical scholarship. This will involve the attempt to discern the historical underpinnings of each mystery. This task is not always an easy one, for a variety of reasons, not the least of which is the absence of any independent historical witness, beyond the Gospels, that attests to the event. We must add to this the fact that the Gospels were not written primarily to record historical data, but rather to increase *faith. They were the first catechisms of Christianity. While this in no way signifies that they ignored history, it does mean that the evangelists' objectives went beyond a simple recounting of facts.*

However, this historical task should not be seen as an impossible undertaking. There are frequently internal factors that point to historicity and support the belief that the events of Jesus' life were not simply woven out of whole cloth.

The second and principal task of this text is spiritual in character. What is this incident, as it appears in one or other of the Gospels, saying to us as Christians today? If the event has been retained and incorporated in the Gospels because it is capable of increasing faith, then the principle task of the scholar in any pastoral sense is to capture that meaning and bring it to light. This task is not as daunting as the first, since it is clearly the intent of the evangelist. But, at the same time, the author's intent may be tiered and multilayered, and to that extent not immediately recognized. It is this latter endeavor that has lent such flavor to the theologian's task today.

THE FIRST MYSTERY
The Baptism of Jesus

*T*he first mystery of light is Jesus' baptism by John the Baptist in the Jordan River. Can we determine its historical circumstances? It comes early in Jesus' ministry and is presented as the first face-to-face meeting between the two end-time figures. It comes relatively late in the ministry of John, although the actual termination of his mission is treated differently in the Synoptic tradition. The baptism is recounted by each of the "Synoptic Gospels"—that is, the Gospels of Matthew, Mark, and Luke (Matt 3:13–17; Mark 1:9–11; Luke 3:21–22).

One contemporary extra-biblical source contains information, albeit brief, about both John and Jesus; this appears in the *Jewish Antiquities* by the Jewish historian of the first century Flavius Josephus. The profile of the two figures as found in Josephus corresponds in large part to what we know from the Gospels. John was an ascetical, charismatic, end-time preacher with a widespread following. Jesus is seen more as a teacher, preacher, and wonder worker, brought to an untimely and cruel death by his opponents. The motivation of Herod for killing John differs from that of the Gospels, centering more on the danger of a popular uprising. But the general outline of each man's life is an important witness to their actual existence. In fact, the widespread popularity of John may explain, at least partially, the evangelists' effort to subordinate him to Jesus throughout the Gospels.

It is only Luke who indicates that John and Jesus were relatives. Their first prenatal contact occurs when Mary visits Elizabeth (Luke 1:39–45), on which occasion John shows deference to Jesus. In no other place in the New Testament, is this relationship even hinted at, and the fact that this appears in the infancy narratives, with their strong theological concerns, raises questions about its historicity. Moreover, John's recognition of Jesus in the womb makes at least problematic the question of his emissaries to Jesus at a much later date: "Are you the one who is to come or shall we look for another?" (Matt 11:2–6).

The Baptism

The focal point of this narrative is the encounter of the two eschatological personalities on the banks of the Jordan. There, in the Synoptic accounts, Jesus was baptized by John and may well have remained part of his company for some time thereafter. There is a single reference to both Jesus and John baptizing at a subsequent time (John 3:22–23), even though there is a later attempt to correct this impression (John 4:1–2). If so, this would point to a similar end-time ministry on the part of both figures. In submitting to John's baptism, Jesus identifies with a sinful people whose deliverance is at hand. At this point we pass from the baptism itself to the trinitarian theophany that is presented as accompanying it. It is the historical question of the baptism itself that must first be addressed.

There are some few strains of evidence in the New Testament that point to a persistent fidelity to John's baptism in the early church. In the Acts of the Apostles, a Christian of the stature of Apollos, a man well versed in Christian teaching, had received only the baptism of John (Acts 18:25). Later at Ephesus, Paul meets disciples who had never heard of the Holy Spirit and had received only John's baptism (Acts 19:1–7).

The question arises, then, as to a possible competitiveness between the followers of the two figures, at least as regards their baptism. What may have been the underlying issue? Since John's baptism was so widespread among the Jews, was it considered sufficient? Why should another baptism be required if one later accepted Christ? Had not

Jesus himself submitted to the baptism of John? Since our evidence is only implied and oblique at best, the question cannot be definitively answered. It may exceed the evidence to speak of a "Johannine sect," but the problem cannot be obscured, especially with the repeated attempts of the New Testament to subordinate John to Jesus at every turn.

The theme of subordination comes to light in the baptismal accounts themselves. With a dependent clause, Luke moves quickly over the baptism itself to highlight the theophany (Luke 3:21–22). In addition, there is the short discussion regarding the appropriateness of John's performing the rite in Matthew's account (Matt 3:13–15). Finally, there is John's reference to the theophany with no reference to the baptism whatsoever (John 1:29–34).

Ironically, all of this presents a strong argument for the historicity of the baptism by John. The evidence points to certain problems in early Christianity. In receiving John's baptism was not Jesus underscoring its efficacy? Yet the emphasis in the early church clearly centered on Jesus' Spirit baptism. Considering the problem involved, had there been no baptism of Jesus by John, the church would hardly have invented it. The fact that it is recorded, even with various nuances, is striking evidence that it must have occurred.

The Theophany

The baptismal narrative is important not only in linking the two eschatological prophets but also as a prototype of Christian baptism. What is immediately suggested in Jesus' immersion in the waters of the Jordan is given explicit expression in the subsequent theophany. Strongly trinitarian in character, the narrative carries us well beyond the original event. By the final years of the first century, the Christian sacrament was conferred with a trinitarian formula (Matt 28:19), even if the earliest formula was "in the name of Jesus" or "Jesus as Lord" (Acts 2:38; 8:16; 10:48). But even this earlier formula would have had trinitarian implications in view of Jesus' intimate relationship with the Father and the Spirit.

Paul teaches that through the death of Jesus we have been reconciled to God and are now at peace. And it is precisely through the conferral of new life, that of the Spirit, that we are incorporated into the life of the Godhead (Rom 5:8–11). What is perhaps the finest summation of the consequences of baptism is found in Galatians 4:1–6. The Father initiates the process by sending his Son as a fully human person ("born of a woman") and a Jew ("under the Law"). This is done in order that those trapped in human ungodliness (the flesh) and the Jews held captive by a death-dealing Law might be liberated. God's salvific work is evidenced in his sharing the Spirit of his risen Son with all the baptized. This constitutes a new relationship, an extension of the family of God, now enabling all believers to address God as *Abba*—father."

This indwelling of the Trinity, so much a part of John's Gospel, is essential to any understanding of the Christian rite.

Trinity and Baptism

Here at the beginning of his earthly ministry, the Father and the Spirit are joined with Jesus in the Synoptics' baptismal theophany. What is presented as a beginning is actually a retrojection of a faith understanding possible only after the resurrection. Jesus stands at the center, the voice of the Father is heard, and the Spirit appears in the form of a dove, the symbol of harmony and peace (cf. Gen 8:8–12), hovering over Jesus.

There are slight differences in each of the accounts. With much of modern scholarship, we see Mark as the earliest of the Gospels, with both Matthew and Luke in dependence on Mark as a source. Mark gives prominence to the baptism in a simple declarative statement, whereas both Matthew and Luke subordinate the baptism grammatically in giving prominence to the theophany. Showing his "universalist" concerns, Luke links the baptism of Jesus with that of "all the people," thus identifying Jesus with those he came to save. In Mark and Luke the words of the Father are directed to Jesus, whereas in Matthew they are directed to a third party, evidently John. In addition, another Lucan characteristic appears with Jesus at prayer at this moment of consecration.

The Mission

The words of the Father are essentially the same in all three accounts. Jesus is identified as "the Son in whom I (the Father) am well pleased." The hovering Spirit is an echo of the Spirit of God frequently presented in the Hebrew

Scriptures as accompanying and empowering a divine commission (Isa 11:2; 42:1; 61:1; 63:9). Jesus is designated the new Israel in being called the "beloved Son," an expression found in the Septuagint of Jeremiah 38:20. In fact, sonship is a frequent designation for Israel in the Old Testament. Matthew dwells at some length on the parallels between Jesus and Israel in both the infancy narratives and the main text of the Gospel. Here, as the baptism is immediately linked with Jesus' desert experience in all three Gospels, Israel's Red Sea–desert experience seems ineluctable.

The sonship of Jesus, however, is not exhausted with the Israel parallel. With his resurrection Jesus was constituted Son of God in the power of the Spirit with a filiation that is totally unique (Rom 1:1–4). The life-giving Spirit is then shared by Christ, empowering the believer. This is activity proper to the Godhead. Jesus is the Son in a way that no other human may claim.

How was this mission of Christ accomplished? It was accomplished through obedient acceptance of the Father's will. It was the obedience that brought Christ to the cross that now earns for him the fullness of Sonship. He is now worthy of the title Lord, a Hebrew surrogate for God himself in the Hebrew Scriptures (Phil 2:8–11). In speaking of Christ as the Son "in whom I am well pleased," there is a clear echo of the first song of the Isaian servant (Isa 42:1). It is this mysterious figure in Isaiah who fulfills a mission that brings him to death and is ultimately extolled by God. He is the obedient one who prefigures Christ himself.

It is this threefold identification of Jesus as Israel, Servant, and Son that is contained in those few verses surrounding the baptism, all of which explains the efficacy of the initiation rite we all receive as Christians. As was said repeatedly in early Christianity, at his baptism Jesus was not purified by the water, rather he gave the waters the power to purify.

The Message

What we have seen is that the moment of Jesus' acceptance of John's baptism has occasioned a catechesis on the meaning of Christian baptism. We are carried beyond the event itself to the presentation of a post-Easter portrait illustrating the significance of this fundamental Christian rite. Baptism derives its efficacy from the willingness of Jesus to undergo his salvific death as the Servant of the Lord. Now "constituted the Son of God in power," he shares his life in God with the baptized, thus making each of us a member of God's household. We now live in the Trinity through the "bond of love," privileged to call the God of the universe our "Abba." This incorporating love of the sacred Trio is actualized in the primary sacrament of initiation, that is, baptism.

The baptism of Jesus is both historical and transhistorical. It begins on the banks of the Jordan between two figures of great spiritual stature. The inauguration of the Messiah's mission then becomes the scaffold for a skillfully painted portrait in which Christian baptism is depicted in terms of the saving work of Jesus and the indwelling of Father, Son, and Spirit.

THE SECOND MYSTERY
The Marriage at Cana

*T*he second of the new mysteries of light added to the Rosary by John Paul II is the wedding feast at Cana, recounted in the second chapter of John's Gospel (John 2:1–11). This engaging account of a village wedding, with its attendant embarrassing inconvenience, has a note of domesticity particularly its own among all the Gospel narratives. More than one commentator has speculated about the propriety of a wedding invitation extended to Jesus and his mother and accepted by all the disciples as well. While not neglecting the story's human appeal, any serious student of John's

*Gospel suspects at once that there must be much
more at stake.*

The Cana narrative appears in John's Gospel and
nowhere else in the four Gospels. That means that we have
no other biblical source with which to compare it. We must
add to that the fact that John's Gospel is highly symbolic
and theological in the deepest sense of the word. This suggests that the author is interested in the account for reasons that are other than historical. John's Christology,
moreover, is the "highest" among the Gospel writers. It is
the risen Christ, now in glory with the Father, who perme-
ates the Gospel as a whole. For theological and literary reasons, it is clear that the first task of the reader is to
determine what the author wished to say through this wedding portrait. While we may feel impoverished in determining the historical kernel of the narrative, we will,
nonetheless, be spiritually enriched in determining the
meaning of the account.

Wedding and Wine

Central to John's teaching is the emphasis on the
inauguration of the end-time or final moment of history in
the person of Jesus of Nazareth. This is the climactic
period of history wherein the Son of God has appeared in
the "flesh" and "has tented" himself among us (1:14). This
beginning of the final period is presented in the terms of
Old Testament eschatological language. Frequently the
final period is presented as marriage in which God defini-

tively takes Israel as his bride (Isa 54:4–8; 62:4–5). Similar imagery often appears in Jesus' parables in a New Testament setting and has its crowning moment in the Book of Revelation, which depicts the marriage of Christ and his bride, the church (Rev 21:2, 9–14). This joy-filled union of God and his people, whether it be Israel or the church, found appropriate expression in that natural union wherein two persons become one in a new community of life. The imagery also works conversely, as in the letter to the Ephesians wherein the exhortation to love and fidelity in marriage is based on the bond of love that unites Christ to his church (Eph 5:21–32).

Seen in this light, the marriage at Cana celebrates symbolically definitive salvation, the final in-gathering of God's people, the messianic era of God's providence. The wine only adds to this notion of end-time fulfillment. Its shortage is introduced by the brief comment of Jesus' mother. "They have no wine." Jesus' response carries a note of noncompliance to his mother's implied request. But, once again, his words must be seen in the light of the narrative as a whole. Jesus' reluctance to act is owing to the fact that his "hour" has not yet come. The "hour" in John's Gospel is the time of his death-resurrection, the decisive and central salvation moment (8:20; 12:23; 13:1). In acquiescing to Mary's request, Jesus anticipates the hour of salvation, which will take place on Calvary. Everything that occurs in the narrative subsequently should be read in the light of Christ's saving death.

Closely connected with end-time thinking in the Old Testament is the notion of an abundance of good food and drink, especially a choice wine (Amos 9:13-14; Isa 25:6-7; Jer 31:12-14). A worthy table or "groaning board" appears as an integral part of the terrestrial presentation of end-time benefits. We have the luxury of speaking of our final destiny in terms that are largely spiritual. Such was not the case during much of pre-Christian times, wherein believers were largely locked into a "this world" perspective.

Seen in this light, the transformation of water into wine at Cana is an important contrast between every day life (water) and the brilliant future that God would provide (wine). The water at Cana stood in six large water jars, intended for use by the Jews in a ritual washing. In substituting the water with wine (the best saved until last), Christ is substituting the abundant wine of New Testament fulfillment for the lifeless and now surpassed waters of Judaism. Again it is John's symbolism that is to the fore. The abundance of wine should really be termed super-abundance—180 gallons! With such an amount, one can only hope that the number is symbolic. On the other hand, how better to express the munificence of God in messianic fulfillment.

Jesus anticipates his "hour," which will come only at the end of John's Gospel. The kingdom of God has arrived, here depicted in terms of a marriage and an abundance of wine. He does this at the request of his mother.

"Woman"

In John's Gospel, Jesus directly addresses Mary on two occasions. In neither does he refer to her as "Mother."

Both at Cana and from the cross, the designation she receives is "Woman." In the case of a son speaking to his mother, the term, while not disrespectful, is at least highly unusual. Since symbolism plays such a significant role in the fourth Gospel, it is a logical question to inquire as to the meaning the author attaches to this designation. The first "woman" to appear in the scriptures is Eve, who is spoken of as the "mother of all living" (Gen 3:20). Not infrequently in early Christian writings, Mary is seen as the new Eve, the mother of the new life in Christ, a symbol of the church itself. In the last book of the Bible, Revelation, a woman again appears; there she is both Israel and the church (Rev 12). As Israel, she gives birth to the Messiah, following which she continues to exist as the church. After the Messiah's birth, she is carried to a desert place where she is witness to the conflict between the serpent (evil) and her own offspring, the members of the church. Therefore the woman of Revelation is both the mother of the Messiah and the church itself as the mother of the Christian reborn. Just as Israel gave birth to the Messiah, so the church gives life to the witnesses of Christ. Mary is then a symbol of both Israel and the church.

In the Cana narrative, Mary is appropriately referred to as "Woman." As the symbol of church, she intercedes with her Son for the end-time blessing of salvation, symbolized by the abundant wine. She makes her request with a total confidence in Jesus' positive response. It is she with whom the beloved disciple, the Christian prototype, will be linked at Calvary and to whose maternal care the disciple is entrusted (John 19:25–27).

The Meaning of Cana

It is not unlikely that Jesus and his companions were at some point in attendance at a wedding feast in Galilee, but it is impossible to determine with any accuracy the circumstances or particulars of such an occasion because whatever the historical situation may have been has been subsumed in a strong eschatological statement. The whole event centers around the person and mission of Christ. In the first chapter of John's Gospel, as the individual disciples become part of Jesus' company, there are ascending degrees of recognition. Jesus is Lamb of God (36), Rabbi (38), Messiah (41), Jesus, son of Joseph (45), Son of God, and King of Israel (49).

Following this crescendo is the climactic account of the wedding feast at Cana. It is at that point that Jesus is presented as heralding the final era of salvation to be realized with his own death-resurrection (his "hour"). It is an account depicted with all the color and brilliance of Old Testament end-time imagery, with a wedding and abundant wine playing an important part. It is the Woman (Israel-church) who requests this final in-breaking on behalf of her needy children. With Christ's response, salvation is anticipated and God's people are provided for—the age of new beginnings is inaugurated. Such a wealth of riches appears early in John's Gospel as a harbinger of what subsequent chapters will illuminate in a series of symbols—light, water, bread—all of which invariably center on the person of Jesus and his saving mission.

THE THIRD MYSTERY

The Announcement of the Kingdom and the Call to Conversion

This mystery of the Rosary centers upon the central theme of Christ's mission: the announcement of the definitive arrival of God's reign and the state of preparedness required for its reception. In the four Gospels, "the kingdom of God" or its equivalent appears approximately fifty times. There is no doubt that end-time anticipation was keen in later Judaism, the so-called inter-testamental period, but the term "kingdom of God" was not common. Its distinctive use in the Gospels probably derives from Christ himself and then became a common feature of early Christian teaching.

The Old Testament Kingdom

What meaning did "the reign of God" have? First of all, its frequent substitution with the "reign of heaven" did not alter its meaning; it simply avoided the use of God's name. This substitution is common, for example, in Matthew's Gospel. From its inception, Israel, unlike its neighbors, was a theocratic state. The only recognized monarch was Yahweh himself, to whom as liberator and conqueror total allegiance was due. This was the God who had led his people from Egypt, covenanted with them on Sinai, and given them the land of Canaan (cf. Exod 15:1–17). When, after the settlement in Canaan, the idea of an earthly king was introduced, it met with considerable opposition (1 Sam 8:6–22); this was primarily due to the fact that it was seen as impinging on the prerogatives of Yahweh. At its best, the establishment of an earthly monarch was a compromise; for reasons of political expediency, the concession was made, but always with the understanding that the king remained subordinate to the overarching sovereignty of the Lord.

In the psalms, Yahweh's kingship is seen in his creation and governance of the universe (Pss 29, 93). While the preeminence of King David remained intact, the experience of human kingship during the monarchical period in Israel brought bitter disappointment and disillusionment. The Books of Kings list the evils done by the kings during the pre-exilic period. This, however, only gave stronger hope to the belief in a future kingdom of peace and justice, presided over by Yahweh as king (Isa 52:7). In the final centuries before Christ, this hope was expressed in apocalyptic terms. In the book of Daniel, after all earthly kingdoms have perished, only the kingdom of God remains (chapter 2).

The Kingdom in Jesus' Preaching

While the *kingdom* may be said to have been a recurring theme in the Old Testament, it was not as dominant or central as *covenant* may be said to have been. The same may be said of its presence in the Dead Sea Scrolls of Qumran. In the case of Jesus, however, it assumes a much stronger role. As Jesus would have envisioned it, the reign signified a restoration of the peace and order of Eden, embracing not only the lower order of creation but also human relations as governed by divine direction. This kingdom was to be presided over by a God of justice whose citizens were to be characterized by a life of uprightness reflective of that of their heavenly prototype. This was a God-centered kingdom wherein human conduct would be wholly measured by covenant fidelity. It was a kingdom, moreover, without boundaries, open to all people of good will, as the ministry of Jesus to the poor and the outcast amply testified.

The New Testament

As Jesus announces that "the reign of God has come near" (Mark 1:15), or is proximate, as in the teaching of John the Baptist (Mark 1:1–8; Matt 3:1–6, 11–12; Luke 3:1–6, 15–18), this reflects not only the proclamation of

Jesus himself but also the understanding of the early church, as the Gospels are composed. It is of great importance to realize that the original teaching of Jesus has been enriched by the understanding in the Holy Spirit, which came to the church only after the resurrection. At that time, the reign of God meant more than in its pre-Easter expression.

All of this is to say that there is now a more comprehensive understanding of the kingdom. It is no longer circumscribed by political or temporal boundaries, but has a wholly religious outlook. It looked to the end of human ills, so closely identified with the realm of evil. It belonged to the age of the Messiah, the longed-for descendant of David. The miracles of Jesus are signs of the kingdom's inauguration in his moving against sin, suffering, and death. In casting out demons and healing the sick, Jesus indicates that the reign of God is present. When asked by John's disciples whether or not he is the promised One, Jesus' answer is implicitly affirmative. The kingdom is present in the blind who see, the deaf who hear, and the poor who are exalted (Matt 11:2–5). The kingdom is present in a new ethic that calls people to an ultra-legal and deeply internal relationship with God. Jesus states that it is no longer necessary to look for signs and wonders, for "the kingdom is among you" (Luke 17:21).

Much of this could have been subsumed by the early church from the teaching of the historical Jesus. But in other areas the church's understanding of the reign of God differs from what Jesus preached. There is no doubt that the kingdom as preached by the apostles and the early Christians was centered in the death-resurrection of

Christ. This salvation event stands at the very center of the reign of God. It is this fuller understanding that is retro-jected into the preaching of the Marcan Jesus, who, in pro-claiming the kingdom, calls for conversion and belief in the Gospel (the "good news"). The "good news" was the *kerygma* (proclamation) of the early church and centered exclusively on the death-resurrection. The early preaching of the church, which proclaimed Jesus as the royal Messiah, viewed this as the result of his being handed over to death and raised up by God. Acceptance of this truth resulted in baptism and the forgiveness of sins (Acts 2:29–41, 3:11–21).

The Present and Future Kingdom

The proclamation of the early church clearly saw the reign of God as a present reality. It was initiated in the presence of the earthly Jesus and amplified with his salvific death. Following the path of humble submission to God's will, he was subsequently exalted and given the title "Lord," thereby becoming the principal agent of salvation (Phil 2:6–11). His kingdom, while not one of this world, had been clearly inaugurated (John 18:36).

What is also clear from the New Testament is the *future* dimension of the kingdom. It would only be defini-tively realized with the return of Christ at the end of time, when all evil will be defeated and all of creation subjected to Christ's lordship (1 Cor 15:23–28). In the present stage of God's reign, there is still pain and suffering, as experi-enced by Christ himself in his ministry, but in the future "every tear will be wiped away." In the presence of impending doom at the Last Supper, Jesus assures his disciples that he will not drink the festive wine until he does so when the "kingdom of God comes" (Mark 14:25; Luke 22:18). As we have seen, wine in abundance was an Old Testament eschatological theme (Isa 25:6). Moreover, at that future date foreigners will take their place at table with Abraham, Isaac, and Jacob (Matt 8:11–12; Luke 13:28–29). It is a kingdom where human lots will be reversed, the privileged ones being the poor, the disconsolate, the meek, and the hungry (Matt 5:3–12; Luke 6:20–23).

This future dimension of the kingdom is sounded in "Thy kingdom come" in both versions of the Lord's Prayer (Matt 6:10; Luke 11:2). In its pre-Easter sense, as taught by Christ, it would have looked toward the full implementation of Israel's spiritual and temporal restoration; in its post-Easter use, it would have looked to the return of the risen Christ on the clouds of heaven as the end-time Son of Man (Mark 13:24–26). This would be followed by the final judgment (Matt 25:31–46), with the subjugation of evildoers and the deliverance of the just.

Conversion

The call to conversion of life accompanied Jesus' announcement of the reign of God. The Greek term for this is *metanoia*. Its Old Testament precedent was the Hebrew *shub*, which basically meant "to turn around on the road, to head in a new direction." This latter term appears more than a thousand times in the Hebrew Bible and more than two hundred times in its religious or moral sense. In other words, the concrete, or physical, meaning was transposed to another key in speaking of a spiritual "change of direction," a reordering of one's life and priorities. Basically it meant moving from a world-centered mentality to an adherence to God's will.

The Old Testament understanding of conversion appears in a variety of passages. It began with a realization of sin's gravity (Ezek 18:23), followed by a complete re-engagement and dedication to Yahweh. This often meant a 180-degree change of direction. None of this was accomplished without God's assistance (Ps 51:9–11; Isa 1:18). The result was a new heart and new spirit. Penitential practices often accompanied conversion, which were later subordinated to a response to social need (Isa 58:6). Its practical expression was an observance of laws and statutes. At the time of the Babylonian exile, conversion was seen as deeply personal and internal (Jer 31:31–34; Ezek 37:26). This change of heart was equally applicable to the individual or the people as a whole.

Repentance, however, included not only a change of heart but a change of mind as well (e.g., Amos 3:10–11; Jer 18:8). More than the center of affectivity, the heart, in Hebrew thought, was the seat of intelligence. No true conversion could take place without a change of attitude. In fact, the Greek *metanoia*, with its inclusion of the word *nous*, or mind, basically means "a change of mind."

The Christian Sense

In the time of John the Baptist and Jesus, conversion was accompanied by a baptismal rite as an external expression of internal change. (Matt 3:5–6; Mark 1:4; Luke 3:3). The earliest call to conversion signified a total gift of oneself to the in-breaking reign of God, a turning from sin in a spirit of total surrender (Matt 3:2–3; 7:13). In its pre-Easter setting, conversion meant conformity to God's Law, a just and upright state of mind. While penitential practices played their part, notably among the disciples of John, they were not a noteworthy feature of Jesus' ministry (Mark 2:18–22).

With the giving of the Spirit in post-Easter times, conversion became inextricably linked with baptism, a rite centering on a total adherence to the lordship of Jesus (Acts 2:38) and actualized by the work of the Spirit within the believer (Acts 2:33; 1 Cor 12:3). There is emphasis on its ongoing character as a process of formation in Christ. The human response centers on the Sermon on the Mount (Matt 5–7). It is a call intended for *all* people (Gal 3:27–28). As an incorporation as well into the body of Christ, the church, it has both an individual and collective sense (Eph 1:22–23).

In summary, then, Christian conversion is dynamic and continuous. Initiated in baptism as a participation in the death and resurrection of the Lord, it is expressed in a death to self in living the life of love, as expressed preeminently in the Sermon on the Mount.

Conversion seeks reconciliation in building up peace with one's neighbor and overcoming every barrier of division.

Conclusion

The close connection between the reign of God and conversion is clear, but this had a different connotation at the various stages of salvation history. It meant one thing to the Hebrew believer, another to the historical figures of Jesus and John, and still another to the Christians of the first century. The common link lay in a change of life and outlook in view of the in-breaking of God's kingdom. The expectation of Christ's early return in the early church, so strong in many pages of the New Testament, gradually receded with the passage of time. In later compositions, for example, John's Gospel, the belief in an early return is not as dominant as in the Synoptic Gospels. Various factors may explain this, one of which was the deeper appreciation of the interim moment. To be a Christian meant to live in Christ, both individually and as church. In one sense, the end had already come, as this intense life in the Spirit was seen as ever more permanent and less transitory. The future return of Christ, never lost sight of, was destined to vindicate his mission before the world. But this presence of Christ was increasingly seen as something not solely in the future but as a very present reality. This had its effect on the eschatological vision.

This third mystery of light in the renewal of the Rosary devotion is an ever present reminder to bring the reign of God to life in our lives, our parishes, and our nation. Every time the cause of justice and peace is served, the kingdom is more present. With every act of inhumanity and selfishness, the reign of God is diminished. If the return of Christ means anything, it is that the final word will be God's. By the gift of the Spirit we have been empowered to build up the kingdom. The call of conversion is a summons to greater fidelity and love, as well as a call to lend our efforts for a more just and human world.

THE FOURTH MYSTERY
The Transfiguration

*T*he fourth mystery of light presents a portrait that is incredibly rich in its message. It offers valuable insights into the multifaceted person of Jesus Christ, ushering us, if only briefly, to the plateau of eternal life. The difficulty arises in trying to uncover the actual historical event. The reason for this is that, like the heavenly intervention surrounding Jesus' baptism, the transfiguration is also a theophany, and theophanies are not easily verifiable in simple historical terms. Theophany literally means "a manifestation of God," or an "in-breaking of God," upon the human scene. In their biblical occurrences, theophanies invariably relay an important mes-

sage. But when it comes to describing an event, that is totally related to a higher sphere, human language is the only device at hand, and language only approximates the meaning of the reality itself.

Legitimate questions can be raised. Was what Matthew calls a "vision" (17:9), granted to the three disciples, something external or purely internal? At what point in Jesus' ministry is it best situated? If before the death of Jesus, how can one explain the doubt and dispersion of the very apostles who had been given the insight? Is it better situated after the resurrection as a further explanation of Jesus' glorified state? These are some of the historical questions that remain unanswered. But none of this detracts from the significance of what is related.

The Transfiguration appears in each of the Synoptic Gospels (Mark 9:2–8; Matt 17:1–8; Luke 9:28–36). There are only slight variations among the three. Again, there are persuasive arguments for seeing Mark as the earliest of the three, the source upon which both Matthew and Luke depend. In the narrative, Jesus takes the three disciples—Peter, James, and John—to a high mountain, where he is transformed in their presence. Coincidentally enough, these are the same disciples who will accompany Jesus to the garden of suffering before his arrest. This transformation is called a metamorphosis by Mark and Matthew—the appearance of Jesus in a completely different form. It is an appearance that anticipates the resurrected Jesus in his post-Easter glory. At this point, there is a claimer from the Father in favor of the Son, as was the case at Jesus' baptism. The transformation then vanishes as quickly as it appeared.

The Vision

There is a time reference in all three Gospels that brings the event into relation with Peter's profession of faith in Jesus at Caesarea Philippi. It is "after six days" in two accounts (Mark 9:2; Matt 17:1) and "after eight days" in one (Luke 9: 28). In the earlier reference, Peter identified Jesus as "the Messiah" (Christ) in Mark and Luke, and as "Christ, the Son of God" in Matthew. At the Transfiguration we return to the identity theme once more. The mountaintop location plays an important role in biblical revelation, but its largely symbolic value renders gratuitous the search for a particular locale.

The heart of the revelation is an appearance of Christ in anticipation of his Easter transformation. At that later time, he was recognized only in faith and therefore not seen by all indiscriminately. He was capable of appearing and disappearing at will, penetrating closed doors, and yet he could be touched and identified and could share a meal with his disciples. At the Transfiguration, his clothes are dazzlingly white, luminous, and transparent; such an appearance often accompanied ethereal figures (Dan 12:3; Mark 16:5; Luke 24:4; Matt 28:3). But this is also a preview of the resurrected body, which is the future lot of the Christian believer (1 Cor 15:40–44; 2 Cor 3:18).

The centrality of Jesus in the vision is accentuated by the presence of two subordinate figures, Moses and

Elijah, representing the Old Testament as pointing to Jesus. Moses represents the Torah, the all-important Law of the Old Testament found in the Bible's first five books, closely identified with the patriarch. Elijah, whose career is recounted in the Books of Kings, represents the tradition of the prophets. In mentioning the two, Mark gives an unexpected priority to Elijah, probably owing to the prophet's importance in the discussion that follows dealing with the belief in Elijah's return (Mark 9:9–13).

The presence of these two biblical personalities enhances Jesus' singular position as the climactic point of salvation history. It is stated that they are involved in discussion with Jesus, but only Luke states the topic of their conversation. They were speaking of Jesus' "exodus," his passage from death to life, his forthcoming passion (Luke 9:30–31). Without the paschal mystery, there could be no future glory, no lasting Transfiguration. Another Lucan characteristic note is the mention of Jesus at prayer when the Transfiguration occurs (9:29); it is true of the Lucan Jesus at every critical moment in his earthly ministry.

The Feast of Tents

Sukkoth, or "Tents," was the joyful harvest feast of the Jewish calendar, during which people lived in small tents to recall God's providence at the time of the exodus. In the course of time, Tents took on an eschatological significance, with the end-time seen as a lasting celebration of the feast recalling God's goodness to his people. In the Transfiguration narrative Peter, overwhelmed by this "glimpse of glory," wants, at all cost, to retain it by building three lasting tents in honor of the three central figures. But this was not to be. Attention must first be directed to the suffering to come (Mark 9:9-13; Matt 17:9-13). The thread of tension between glory and pain is woven intricately into the fabric of the Transfiguration account.

The Heavenly Voice

As was the case at the baptism, God's recognition of Christ as his Son appears again at the Transfiguration. The *shekinah*, or heavenly cloud, was the unmistakable sign of God's providential care, reflecting his glory (Exod 16:10) and his abiding presence (Exod 40:34).

In the three Synoptic Gospels (Matthew, Mark, and Luke) the Father speaks in the third person, the message addressed to the three apostles. His words contain three scriptural allusions, all related to the life and mission of Jesus. In the Old Testament both Israel (Hos 11:1) and the king (Ps 2:7) are spoken of as God's son, with the latter also assuming messianic overtones. The words on this occasion say all of that and more. Here they underscore Christ's unique and singular sonship, realized fully in the glory of his Spirit-filled resurrection (Rom 1:1-4). In being designated as "my chosen" (Luke) or "my beloved" (Mark) or the one "in whom I am well pleased" (Matt), the reference is to Isaiah's servant of the Lord (Isa 42:1), whose spirit of submission ultimately brought him to suffering and death. The admonition "Listen to him" strongly suggests the promised prophet like Moses (Deut 18:15), who was also an end-time figure in Jewish eschatology.

The words are a succinct summary of the entire mission of Jesus, who was the servant of the Lord in his saving death, the prophet like Moses in his message, and the glorified Son of God in his resurrection.

The Teaching

The "glimpse of glory" ends as quickly as it began. But, as we have seen, its message encapsulates the whole of Jesus' salvific destiny. As the personal Son of God, his influence and divine prerogatives will be fully experienced only with his rising from death. But it is not simply a vision of unmatched joy or Peter's feast of Tents. The Transfiguration has suffering deeply etched in its presentation. Even the personalities betray the future; they are the same three who will be with Jesus in the garden of suffering. It is little wonder that Peter's desire to prolong the glory in the building of three tents receives scant attention. The conversation of the three heavenly figures says it all. They are taken up with Jesus' exodus, his passage through the crucible of suffering at the Father's behest. In fact, it is the Father himself who supports their words in his message of suffering as well as glory.

The second letter of Peter refers to the Transfiguration as a transforming moment (2 Pet 1:16–18). Stories and edifying tales can serve a worthy purpose. Sometimes they illustrate a truth, clarify a proposition, or give added motivation. But nothing can compare with the power and the glory of Christ's truth. Christ is not only the object of our admiration; he is the source of our ability to become like unto him. As we reverence him as Son of God and Lord of history, we are forever reminded of the fact that he was the Lord's Servant, who carried the cross of pain, rejection, and discouragement. In short, whether in sorrow or in joy, Christ remains the model of our lives.

It is an inestimable grace. The old covenant has been superseded by the new. The glory of the former covenant, reflected in Moses' refulgent face, has now passed from the scene. It has been surpassed by the lasting glory of the new (2 Cor 3:7–11). And it is all so intensely *personal*. With our gaze fixed on the glory of Christ, we, too, are being transfigured. In a metamorphosis that is ongoing, we are transformed from glory to glory through the action of the Spirit within us (2 Cor 3:8). So empowered, we continue and never surrender. Ever open to growth and transformation, we desire "what is good, pleasing, and perfect." (Rom 12:2).

As the group descends from the mountaintop, Jesus enjoins the three not to speak of what they have seen until after the resurrection. Suffering must come first. And so it is for all of us. But that "glimpse of glory" reminds us of the future that no one can take from us.

THE FIFTH MYSTERY
The Last Supper and the Eucharist

Appropriately, the five new mysteries of the Rosary conclude with the remembrance of Christ's final meal with his disciples during which the gift of the Eucharist is conferred. The two sacraments that appear indisputably in the New Testament are baptism and the Eucharist. The antiquity of the Eucharistic tradition is clear from Paul's claim, in writing to the Corinthians in the early fifties, that this is tradition that he is transmitting as already fixed in the life of the church (1 Cor 11: 23–26). This constitutes a written witness to the sacrament, stemming from a period within a decade or so after the resurrection.

A Passover Supper?

Each of the Synoptic Gospels places the Last Supper and the death of Christ on the feast of Passover. With the day beginning on the evening before, this would place the supper/death on Thursday/Friday. John, on the other hand, describes both of the events as occurring prior to the Passover, which that year would have been celebrated on Friday/Saturday. He states that Jesus' body had to be taken down from the cross before sundown, the beginning of the Passover observance. This would mean that the final meal in John's Gospel was simply a farewell dinner of Jesus with his disciples. Efforts to reconcile the dates of the two traditions have not met with success. Both could be based on theological rather than historical premises, since there is logic in seeing the saving death of Jesus as related to the Passover tradition. From a historical point of view, there is more logic to John's position than the Synoptics. This avoids the difficulty of a trial, sentencing, and execution of Jesus on one of the most sacred days of the Jewish calendar.

What *is* certain in all the Gospels is the connection between the liberation of the Hebrew people from Egyptian servitude and the saving death of Jesus.

Once the Passover setting is in place in the Synoptic tradition, the Jewish feast is quickly lost sight of. Were it not for Luke's mention of the third cup of wine after dinner, we would not even be able to determine a point in the ritual when the Eucharist took place. The formalized account of the institution is simply inserted into the narrative with no advertence to the stages of the Passover ritual. In fact, in the Lucan account the words over the bread come early in the meal and those over the cup only after the meal is finished. The Jewish feast serves mainly as a backdrop to the account of Eucharistic institution.

Early Church Liturgy

The words of institution of the Eucharist appear four times in the New Testament (Mark 14:22–25; Matt 26:26–29; Luke 22:19–20; 1 Cor 11:23–26). The four accounts actually reflect two different formulas, one shared by Mark and Matthew, the other by Luke and Paul. From a compositional point of view, this would mean that, within the context of Jesus' Last Supper with his disciples, the Gospel tradition has inserted a liturgical formula already in use in the early church. Since there are two formulas recounted, they probably represent the liturgy of two different churches, perhaps Jerusalem and Antioch.

Symbols and Words

In the words of Jesus, the bread and wine are representative of his body and blood. In their distinct and separate state, they represent Christ in a state of death. It is an atoning death, as the accompanying words make clear, less clearly stated in the case of the bread than of the cup. Only Luke and Paul indicate that the body "is given over for you."

In Mark and Matthew, the words over the cup follow immediately; in Luke and Paul, the meal separates the two. This variation does not have major consequences, since both formulas telescope the institution account in a very concise and compact manner. There is no attempt here at an historical replay. In the reference to "blessing" and "giving thanks," the Father is acknowledged and praised as the sacred action takes place.

The words over the wine have clear scriptural significance. It is seen as covenant blood in *all* the Gospel accounts, with Luke and Paul making specific reference to the "new covenant." The language is that of *sacrifice*. It distinctly echoes the words of Moses, who, in ratifying the covenant on Mount Sinai, holds the container of animal blood aloft and says, "See the blood of the covenant" (Exod 24:8). He then splashes some of the sacrificial blood on the altar (signifying Yahweh) and also sprinkles the people. In Hebrew thought, life was in the blood, thus cementing the new relationship between God and people. Jesus, therefore, subsumes the action of Sinai in establishing a new and lasting covenant in fulfillment of the words of Jeremiah: "The days are surely coming, says the Lord, when I will make a new covenant with the house of Israel and the house of Judah...But this is the covenant that I will make...I will put my law within them, and I will write it on their hearts; and I will be their God, and they shall be my people. No longer shall they teach one another, or say to each other, 'Know the Lord,' for they shall all know me" (Jer 31:31, 33–34).

Both the sign and the words of institution speak of Christ's sacrificial death. As animal blood sealed the Sinai covenant, so the blood of Christ seals its New Testament counterpart. But, in line with the promise of

Jeremiah, the new covenant effects what the earlier intended but failed to realize. It is written not in stone but on the human heart. What characterizes the new covenant is its strong interiority; it touches the soul directly and elicits a profoundly personal response. It is small wonder that New Testament writers saw the Jeremiah prophecy uniquely realized in Christ.

The Synoptics speak of the blood that is poured out for "the many," with Matthew adding, "for the forgiveness of sins," in language that is clearly sacrificial. While the immediate reference is to Jesus' action at the Last Supper, the liturgical formula used points to the ongoing "replay" of the Eucharist in the life of the church. This note is clearly struck in the rubric "Do this in remembrance of me" (Luke 22:19; 1 Cor 11:24).

Each time the Eucharist is offered, it brings before the Father in a sacred sign the once-for-all death of the Lord on Calvary. This is not a question of many sacrifices; the offering of Christ is single and nonrepeatable (Heb 10:10–18). What the Eucharist does is make that single offering accessible to believers in all ages in deepening that covenant of the heart.

The Kingdom of God

"Truly I tell you, I will never again drink of the fruit of the vine until that day when I drink it new in the kingdom of God" (Mark 14:25; cf. Matt 26:29; Luke 22:18). This reference to Christ's continuation of table fellowship with his disciples looks to the future dimension of God's reign, the time of the kingdom's full implementation. As was said in our treatment of the third mystery of light (the proclamation and call to conversion), in the teaching of Jesus there is both a present and future reign of God: in the present case the reference is clearly of the future. It is only tangentially related to the institution formula and can be viewed as part of Jesus' original Last Supper discourse. It strikes a note of sadness and a painful hiatus. With his ministry, which was not markedly successful, drawing to a close and in the face of impending tragedy, Jesus shared a final meal with his companions, still confident that God's reign will triumph. This does not mean that he saw the future with clarity. The extent of Christ's knowledge during his life "in the flesh" remains uncertain. But he remained confident that his role as God's emissary would not end in failure. In drawing on the eschatological imagery of an end-time banquet, he promises his disciples a felicitous and joyful outcome to the present trial.

The Historical Supper

There is no doubt about the primitive church's understanding of Jesus' saving death and its eucharistic commemoration. But can we get below this layer of thought to determine what the historical Jesus intended at this final meal with his friends. Considering the importance that this event assumed in the life of early Christianity, there can be no doubt that its origins go back to Jesus himself. At the same time, the eucharistic action reflects a post-Easter understanding of Jesus' mission and his continued presence in the elements of bread and wine. This is a mystery only understood through a faith made possible by the Spirit of the risen Christ.

Having said that, we can also understand how the symbolic action could proceed from Jesus during his earthly life. Symbols were common in the life of the prophets. More than mere signs, they were understood to contain in some way what they signified. Jeremiah carries the yoke on his shoulders as a meaningful sign of the people's future subjection to Babylonian rule (ch. 27). The two baskets of good and bad fruit signify deliverance and punishment for the Jewish people (ch. 24). These symbols were not mere indicators or suggestions of possibility. In their inevitability they were pregnant with meaning.

So, too, at the final supper, Jesus places in strong relief the separated elements of bread and wine, a symbolic presentation of the forthcoming tragedy of his death. In this moment of intense sadness, he speaks in an eloquent sign of impending doom, but is also quick to add a note of future vindication when the kingdom is fully inaugurated. None of this would be beyond the understanding of his disciples in view of their religious and cultural background. By the same token, it does not require a post-Easter understanding of the glorified Christ ubiquitously present in time and place. Nor does it demand that Christ's original words contain a sacrificial connotation. The later understanding would simply build on the first, retaining a genuine continuity in meaning.

Praying the Mystery

In a real sense, the fifth mystery of light is *climactic*. It brings together all the mysteries that precede—Joyful, Sorrowful, Glorious, and Light-filled. The Eucharist, as the Second Vatican Council (1962–1965) stated, stands at the very heart of Christian belief and is our noblest form of prayer. In it we affirm and live the saving death of Christ until he comes again. As a community and as individuals, we renew our covenant commitment, reasserting our belief in that sacred bond with our God, which makes of us a sacred people, a royal priesthood. As the new and eternal covenant, it reaches the very depth of our being and elicits a response of heartfelt gratitude. It is no longer the covenant of old, with its decalogue of hallowed memory. This is a covenant that finds its measure in the Sermon on the Mount (Matt 5:1–7:27), going well beyond negative prohibition or sanctioned command. Resting on a higher level, it seeks the good of others at every turn.

In the Eucharist we find forgiveness of sins, that reconciliation for which Christ was missioned (2 Cor 5:18–21). It is that sacrifice which, both ever ancient and ever new, is offered for us and our transgressions.

Sacraments are *not* merely signs. Christian tradition is eminently clear on that. Biblically, a simple sign flies in the face of the Judaeo-Christian tradition. Sacraments effect what they signify, and none more so than the Eucharist. Theology will discuss the "how" of this reality, but it cannot deny the *fact*. Calvary is constantly made present to bring Christ's single saving act to life at every time and in every place.

The Eucharist is offered in anticipation of the heavenly banquet to which we are all invited. It calls us to attentiveness and preparedness. No one enters the banquet hall without being properly attired (Matt 22:11–13). Covenant commitment must find expression in daily life and conduct. The Eucharist serves as both a summons and a source of strength.

In the narrative of the Eucharist we are brought into contact with its origin and its earliest lived experience in tradition. We return with Christ to the upper room, but we also see the early church at worship. Both are meaningful. We live in Christ and in the church. Our recitation of the Mysteries of Light reminds us of both.

For Further Reading

Anonymous hermitess. *The New Luminous Mysteries of the Rosary: Scriptural Meditations for Pope John Paul II's Mysteries of Light*

Boadt, Lawrence. *Reading the Old Testament*

Brown, Raymond. *101 Questions and Answers on the Bible*

Flannagan, Patrick J. *The Gospel of Mark Made Easy*

Marrow, Stanley B. *The Gospel of John*

Miller, John W. *Meet the Prophets*

Montague, George T. *Understanding the Bible*

Perkins, Pheme. *Reading the New Testament*

Powell, Mark Allen. *What Are They Saying About Luke?*

Senior, Donald. *What Are They Saying About Matthew?*

Senior, Donald et al. *Invitation to the Gospels*

Zanchettin, Leo (editor). *Matthew: A Devotional Commentary*

ILLUMINATIONBOOKS

Some Other Books in the Series

Little Pieces of Light...Darkness and Personal Growth
by Joyce Rupp

The Love that Keeps Us Sane
by Marc Foley, O.C.D.

The Threefold Way of Saint Francis
by Murray Bodo, O.F.M.

Living Simply in an Anxious World
by Robert J. Wicks

Hear the Just Word & Live It
by Walter J. Burghardt, S.J.

Everyday Virtues
by John W. Crossin, O.S.F.S.

Why Are You Worrying?
by Joseph W. Ciarrocchi

God Lives Next Door
by Lyle K. Weiss

Joy, The Dancing Spirit of Love Surrounding You
by Beverly Elaine Eanes

Following in the Footsteps of Jesus
by Gerald D. Coleman, S.S. and David M. Pettingill